D0475334

ULTIMATE MILITARY MACHINES

SUBMARINES

Tim Cooke

Smart Apple Media

This edition published in 2013 by
Smart Apple Media, an imprint of Black Rabbit Books
PO Box 3263, Mankato, MN 56002

www.blackrabbitbooks.com

© 2012 Brown Bear Books Limited

Brown Bear Books Ltd.
Editorial Director: Lindsey Lowe
Managing Editor: Tim Cooke
Children's Publisher: Anne O'Daly
Picture Manager: Sophie Mortimer
Picture Researcher: Andrew Webb
Creative Director: Jeni Child

Library of Congress Cataloging-in-Publication Data

Submarines / edited by Tim Cooke.
     p. cm. -- (Ultimate military machines)
 Includes index.
 Audience: Grades 4-6.
 ISBN 978-1-59920-822-0 (library binding)
 1. Submarines--Juvenile literature. I. Cooke, Tim, 1961-
 VM365.S75 2013
 623.825'7--dc23
                          2012007409

Printed in the United States of America at Corporate Graphics, North Mankato, Minnesota

Picture Credits

Front Cover: U.S. Navy

BAe Systemsl: 28t; John Batchelor: 06/07; National Defence, Canada: 19tl; PLAN: 27br; Robert Hunt Library: 07cr, 07br,
09tr, 13b, 16, 20, 21tl, 22cl, 23tl, 23br, 24tr, 24bl; TopFoto: Ullstein Bild 21br; U.S. Department of Defense: 05b, 10cl, 12cl,
12bc, 14tr, 15tr; U.S. Navy: 04, 06br, 08, 09b, 10br, 11cl, 11br, 13t, 14bl, 15bl, 17tl, 17bl, 18cl, 18cr, 19cr, 22br, 25tr, 25b,
26, 27tl, 29tl; Voyenno-Morskoyflot Rossii 28/29; Windmill Books: 05tl.

Key: t = top, c = center, b = bottom, l = left, r = right.

All Artworks: Windmill Books.

PO1559
10-2012

9 8 7 6 5 4 3 2

CONTENTS

INTRODUCTION

Deep beneath the oceans lurk some of the most powerful modern weapons: submarines. Nuclear-powered submarines patrol the seas, staying underwater for weeks at a time before they emerge to strike fear in the enemy.

USS KEY WEST

Tower, or sail, of submarine

Periscope for seeing above water when submerged

STRIKE FORCE

The U.S. Navy's underwater strike force includes Los Angeles class nuclear-powered attack subs like the USS *Key West*. In service since 1987, the submarine carried out attacks against Afghanistan in 2001.

SPECIFICATIONS

Crew: 14 officers, 126 enlisted
Length: 361.9 ft (110.3 m)
Beam: 33 ft (10 m)
Propulsion: 1 x nuclear reactor, 1 shaft
Max Speed: 21 kts
Displacement: 6,900 tons (6,260 t)
Armament: 16 missile tubes

SUBMARINE: A vessel that can operate under the sea.

ORIGINS

Submerging powerful weapons underwater might seem like a modern idea. In fact, military submarines are over 200 years old. During the American Revolution (1775–1783), inventors came up with ways of "sailing" beneath the water.

TURTLE

In 1776 American inventor David Bushnell used his egg-shaped wooden vessel, *Turtle* (left), to try to sink the British warship HMS *Eagle*. He failed, but the military submarine was born.

WORLD WARS

Subs played a key role in both world wars. In World War I (1914–1918), German U-boats sank supply ships in the Atlantic. In World War II (1939–1945), U.S. submarines in the Pacific helped force the Japanese to surrender.

▲ A German U-boat patrols the North Atlantic in World War II; the U-boats targeted merchant ships.

U-BOAT: Short for "Unterseeboot," a German submarine.

WHAT'S A SUBMARINE?

Submarines, or subs, are ocean-going vessels that operate fully under the water's surface. A modern submarine can remain underwater for months without surfacing. As well as carrying weapons, they have to carry all the supplies the crew might need.

SILENT SERVICE

Hidden submarines approach silently and attack without warning. Huge vessels patrol the oceans, carrying ballistic or nuclear missiles. They can strike targets from hundreds of miles away.

Tower or sail is the only part of the submarine visible above the water

USS SEAWOLF

Torpedoes stored on board

Hull made from strong steel

▲ The crew of the USS *Thresher*, one of the U.S. Navy's first nuclear attack subs, died in 1963 when the sub sank during sea trials.

BALLISTIC: A long-range, unmanned projectile.

USS *SEAWOLF*

The fastest tactical submarines in the U.S. Navy are the Seawolf class. Their job is to attack enemy submarines. The *Seawolf* carries 130 crew on board.

SHORT OF SPACE

A large submarine is about 550 feet (168 m) long and 40 feet (12.2 m) wide. Most of the space is needed to store weapons and supplies, or for engines, so the crew fit in wherever there is space. Sometimes they have to sleep next to the missiles.

Bunks for the crew

Propeller.

X-CRAFT AND *TIRPITZ*

Even tiny submarines can be deadly. In September 1943, during World War II, the British targeted the German battleship *Tirpitz*. Six X-Craft midget subs (top right) sailed to Norway. Each had a crew of just six men. They found and attacked the *Tirpitz* (right). The damage kept the battleship out of the war for a year.

TACTICAL: Relating to smaller, short-term operations against the enemy.

SUBMARINE MISSION

Submarines can be both tactical and strategic weapons. As tactical weapons, they can destroy specific enemy ships. In a strategic role, submarines use their long-range weapons to threaten any enemy with an attack.

COAST CLEAR

An officer on the attack submarine USS *Norfolk* checks the ocean surface through a periscope. If there are no hostile vessels, the submarine will rise to the surface.

HUNT 'N' KILL

The U.S. Navy's fast attack submarines are tactical weapons. These "hunter-killers" carry torpedoes and missiles. Their task is to sink enemy ships.

PERISCOPE: A tube with mirrors for observing the ocean surface.

► By operating in small groups, submarines can increase their firepower.

"Of all branches of men in the forces, there is none which shows more devotion and faces grimmer perils than submariners."
SIR WINSTON CHURCHILL

MISSILE PLATFORM

A key job of submarines like USS *Memphis* (below) is to fire long-range missiles. Nuclear missiles are strategic weapons that threaten a whole country. Nonnuclear missiles are used to destroy military targets.

NUCLEAR: Creating energy by splitting atoms or bashing them together.

NUCLEAR WEAPONS

Submarine missiles can be fitted with nuclear warheads. No one wants to fire them. They act as a deterrent, so that the enemy does not attack.

BALLISTIC MISSILES

A ballistic missile fired from a submarine explodes over the ocean. Long-range missiles from submarines can strike at virtually any target, on land or sea.

▼ A Tomahawk cruise missile is launched from the USS *La Jolla*, a nuclear-powered attack submarine.

CRUISE MISSILES

Long-range cruise missiles can be nuclear or conventional. Conventional missiles are nonnuclear. They take out military targets. Nuclear missiles could wipe out whole cities. They are used as a deterrent.

DETERRENT: A threat that stops someone from acting.

OTHER ROLES

Submarines are not only missile platfoms. They are used for research, transportation, or patrolling the seas. They are ideal for secret missions, such as spying.

SECRET STRIKE

Submarines are a great way to deliver special forces for secret missions. Here, a U.S. Navy SEAL leaves a sub to make his way to a rigid rubber craft (RRC) on the surface.

Research submarines are used to test new military equipment. They can also gather information about the enemy. They are vital for monitoring the environmental health of the oceans and the seabed.

SEAL DELIVERY

HELPING OUT

The submersible *Mystic* is carried on the deck of a larger sub. Such deep-sea rescue vessels are used when subs get trapped, even at depths of 5,000 feet (1,535 m).

SUBMARINE FIREPOWER

Submarines carry weapons designed to attack and destroy targets at sea and on land. Torpedoes and missiles are long-distance weapons. Mines blow up closer targets.

TRIDENT

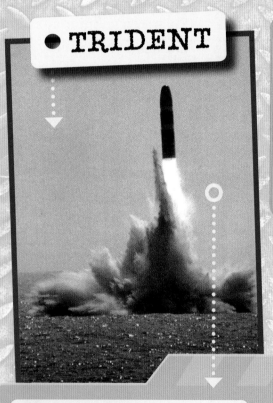

NUCLEAR REDUCTION

In the 1970s, the Strategic Arms Limitation Talks reduced the number of nuclear weapons held around the world. Under the terms of the agreement, the U.S. Navy got rid of many of its nuclear weapons.

POSEIDON

TRIDENT

A Trident ballistic missile is launched from the USS *Nevada*. Trident can hit targets as far as 4,000 miles (6,400 km) away and has more than one warhead.

◀ The USS *Will Rogers* submarine launches a Poseidon C-3 ballistic missile. The Poseidon was used by NATO for over 40 years.

WARHEAD: The explosive part of a missile.

TORPEDOES

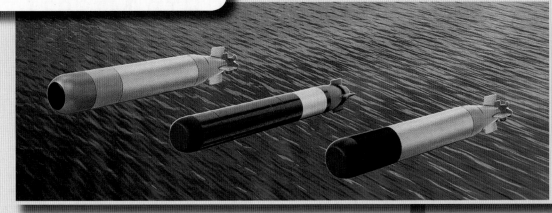

Torpedoes travel through the water. They can hole a ship below the waterline, causing it to sink as the water rushes in. They are driven by an electric motor at the back and steered by a guidance system in the center. The front holds the explosives.

▲ Since the early 20th century, various torpedoes have been the main strike weapons on submarines.

▲ The crew of a surfaced U-boat watches as a merchant ship the sub has torpedoed sinks beneath the water.

WORLD WAR II

From 1940 to 1943, German U-boats sank 20 percent of Allied supply ships. Their success almost starved Britain into surrender. The Allies began sailing in guarded convoys.

CONVOY: A group of vessels or vehicles all traveling in formation.

MISSILE READY

As technology has advanced, missiles have become the most widely used submarine weapons. Vessels do not even have to surface to fire their missiles. They can be fired from deep beneath the war to hit distant targets.

● SHIP MISSILE

● TOMAHAWK

SUBHARPOON

Subharpoons are radar-guided anti-ship missiles. They can hit targets up to 80 miles (128 km) away. Guided by radar, they are hard to spot because they fly close to the surface of the sea.

◀ A Tomahawk cruise missile speeds away after being launched from a submarine. Subs can carry dozens of missiles and launch them virtually simultaneously.

RADAR: A detection system that works by using radio waves.

SENSORS

When they are submerged, submarines rely on sensor systems to "see" what is happening above the water. Crew on the control deck watch radar screens for signs of enemy vessels.

▲ Sonar technicians listen on headphones on the guided-missile destroyer the USS *The Sullivans.* Sonar uses sound waves to locate underwater objects. It is used to listen for enemy submarine activity but also for the sounds of marine mammals.

SEA MINES

Some submarines release sea mines. These floating bombs explode if enemy ships or submarines touch their prongs, or if a passing vessel changes the water pressure.

SONAR: A tracking system that uses sound to detect activity.

SUBMARINE CREW

Living on a submarine doesn't suit everyone. The crew must go without daylight or fresh air. They have to live in cramped conditions without feeling claustrophobic. They also have to get along with their colleagues.

SILENCE PLEASE

Submariners also have to be able to be quiet. When two submarines stalk each other, the slightest sound can give them away. Even the turn of a screw is enough for an enemy sonar operator to work out a sub's position.

LISTENING HARD

During World War II, a German U-boat crewmember listens for an enemy ship overhead. Submarine engines were noisier then, but sonar equipment was also far more basic.

CLAUSTROPHOBIC: Not liking enclosed spaces.

◀ The crew is on watch in the main control center.

"Knowing the types of sounds and what to listen for takes skill."
JOHN ROONEY, PETTY OFFICER, IST CLASS

SEA STALKER

The *Seawolf* is the U.S. Navy's fastest tactical submarine. Its 130 crewmembers are specially trained to locate and attack other submarines.

SEA TRIALS

The crew takes position on the sail and deck of the USS *Seawolf* during trials in 2002.

WATCH: A naval word for a shift, or a period of time spent at work.

SUBMARINE JOBS

Everyone on a submarine has a specific role. The crew are split into departments, commanded by the Executive Department. Engineering looks after the engines; Combat Systems is in charge of weapons. Navigation and Operations steers the ship and handles communications. Submarine training is more demanding than for most other armed forces.

▲ The captain of a World War II submarine looks through the periscope for enemy activity.

"Submariners are a bunch of intelligent misfits that somehow seem to get along, understand each other and work well together."
OVERHEARD SUBMARINE OFFICER

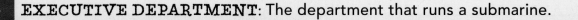

EXECUTIVE DEPARTMENT: The department that runs a submarine.

Engineers work in the engine room of an Upholder class Royal Canadian Navy submarine. The Upholder has a diesel–electric engine. They are cheaper to build than nuclear engines, but they are noisier and not as efficient.

▶ Submariners practice in a dive simulator at the Trident Training Facility at Kings Bay, Georgia.

USS KENTUCKY

Crew members look out from the sail of USS *Kentucky*. The Ohio class ballistic missile submarine has been in service since 1991.

DIVE SIMULATOR: A training center for operating submarines.

SUBMARINE HISTORY

Since the start of the 20th century, submarines have played a vital role in warfare. They helped bring both world wars to a speedier end. Today they still have a vital role to play in both defense and attack.

WWI U-BOAT

Early submarines were very uncomfortable. The working and living spaces were even more cramped than they are today. They were cold and damp, and had no washing facilities.

◀ Crewmen in the engine room of a U-boat in World War I. The whole boat smelled of engine oil.

DETONATION: The action of a bomb exploding.

LUSITANIA SUNK

The British passenger liner *Lusitania* left New York for Britain on May 1, 1915. Days later, the Germans declared unrestricted war at sea. U-boat U-20 torpedoed the *Lusitania*, which sank. Only 764 of the 1,959 people on board survived.

EYEWITNESS

"Shot struck [the] starboard side close behind the bridge. An extraordinary heavy detonation followed, with a very large cloud of smoke..."
CAPT SCHWIEGER OF U-20

WORLD WAR I

Among the victims of the sinking of the *Lusitania* were 123 American passengers. Their deaths led to a public outcry in the United States. That single hit by a German torpedo was the catalyst for the Americans entering World War I on the side of the Allies.

▲ This painting shows the German U-53 sinking the Norweigan cargo vessel *Asheim* in 1917.

CATALYST: Something that makes something else happen.

WORLD WAR II

At the start of World War II, German U-boats attacked Allied supply routes in the Atlantic and Mediterranean. After 1941, the action moved to the Pacific. U.S. submarines sank Japanese supply vessels.

"No attempt of any kind must be made to rescue members of ships sunk."
ADMIRAL DÖNITZ, ORDERS TO U-BOATS, 1942

U-boats at a German naval dockyard. Early in the war, the U-boats enjoyed great success against Allied merchant shipping. Their crews called the period the "Happy Time."

SILENT KILLERS

World War II submarines ran on batteries, because electric engines made almost no noise. The main engine recharged the batteries when the sub was sailing on the surface.

A U.S. submarine prepares to dive in the Pacific. The defeat of the Japanese Navy left Allied subs free to sink merchant supply ships, leaving the Japanese islands starving.

MERCHANT SHIPS: Unarmed vessels used to carry cargo.

◀ *U-112* surfaces to attack a merchant ship with its guns. Commanders kept torpedoes for attacking warships from underwater.

U-BOAT LIFE

A U-boat crew plays cards to pass the time. Submarine life was uncomfortable, boring, and potentially dangerous. Torpedoes, depth charges, and bombs were a constant threat.

Many people's idea of life on a submarine comes from the famous German movie, *Das Boot* (1981). The film tells the story of the crew of U-96. It was a realistic portrayal of life on a U-boat in World War II.

DEPTH CHARGE: An underwater bomb that blows up at a set depth.

FALKLANDS

In 1982 Great Britain went to war when Argentina invaded the Falkland Islands, a tiny British territory in the South Atlantic. Submarines played a key part in the 74-day war that won the islands back for Britain.

> "We, as professionals, said it was just too bad that we lost the Belgrano."
> ARGENTINE REAR ADMIRAL ALLARA

▲ Holed beneath the water, the *General Belgrano* starts to sink on May 2, 1982.

▲ HMS *Conqueror* flies the skull and crossbones after sinking the *Belgrano*.

SUNK

Britain's nuclear-powered attack submarine HMS *Conqueror* sank the Argentine cruiser *General Belgrano* with two torpedoes. More than 320 crew died. Fearing more sub attacks, the Argentine navy stayed in port for the rest of the conflict, which helped Britain gain victory.

CRUISER: The most powerful type of modern warship.

MODERN WARS

Submarines were used in Operation Enduring Freedom, the 2001 U.S.-led invasion of Afghanistan. From hundreds of miles away, submarines launched Tomahawk cruise missiles at targets linked with the Taliban and with al-Qaeda terrorists.

▼ The USS *Louisville* passes under the Golden Gate Bridge in San Francisco.

NEW SUPPLIES

Nuclear submarines can stay underwater for months, but eventually they have to be resupplied. They meet up with supply ships to stock up without having to return to harbor.

▲ USS *Greeneville* resurfaces at sea to take on food, supplies, and personnel.

GALLERY

The biggest submarine fleet in the world belongs to the United States. However, many other countries also operate submarines, including Russia, China, Britain, and France.

USS *LOUISIANA*

The *Louisiana* is one of 18 Ohio-class ballistic-missile submarines. The Ohio class forms the main U.S. nuclear deterrent. They have such a long range they can launch ballistic missiles from any of the world's seas at targets on any continent.

SPECIFICATIONS

Crew: 15 officers, 140 enlisted
Length: 353.3 ft (107.7 m)
Max Speed: 25 knots
Displacement: 18,750 tons (17,010 tonnes)

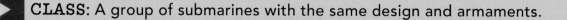

CLASS: A group of submarines with the same design and armaments.

USS TOLEDO

The *Toledo* is a Los Angeles class nuclear-powered fast attack submarine. The class is often used to escort warships and carriers.

SPECIFICATIONS
Crew: 13 officers, 116 enlisted
Length: 360 ft (109.7 m)
Max Speed: 30 knots
Displacement: 6,927 tons (6,284 tonnes)

TYPE 093

SPECIFICATIONS
Crew: Fewer than 100
Length: 360.9 ft (110 m)
Max Speed: 35 knots
Displacement: 6,614–7,716 tons (6,000–7,000 tonnes)

The Shang-class nuclear-powered attack submarine is the latest addition to the Chinese naval fleet. It carries torpedoes and antiship missiles.

DISPLACEMENT: A vessel's size, measured by how much water it moves.

GALLERY

🇬🇧 HMS VANGUARD

SPECIFICATIONS
Crew: 143 total
Length: 490 ft (149.35 m)
Max Speed: 25 knots
Displacement: 15,865 tons
  (14,392 tonnes)

Britain uses the Vanguard class of nuclear-powered submarines as its nuclear deterrent. At least one of Britain's four Vanguard submarines is at sea at all times, armed with Trident ballistic missiles.

SPECIFICATIONS
Crew: 130
Length: 557.7 ft (170 m)
Max Speed: 29 knots
Displacement: 14,720 tons
  (13,354 tonnes)

TRIDENT: A ballistic missile armed with a nuclear warhead.

The Virginia class is a new generation of submarine. It carries out escort and attack functions and was designed to be cheaper than its predecessors.

SPECIFICATIONS

Crew: 113
Length: 377 feet (115 m)
Max Speed: 25 knots
Displacement: 7,800 tons
(7,076 tonnes)

The Borei class is the newest type of nuclear-powered ballistic missile submarine built for the Russian Navy.

BOREI CLASS

GLOSSARY

ballistic: A long-range, unmanned projectile.

catalyst: Something that makes something else happen.

class: A group of submarines with the same design and armaments.

claustrophobic: Not liking enclosed spaces.

convoy: A group of vessels or vehicles all traveling in formation.

cruiser: The most powerful type of modern warship.

depth charge: An underwater bomb that blows up at a set depth.

deterrent: A threat that stops someone from acting.

detonation: The action of a bomb exploding.

displacement: A vessel's size, measured by how much water it moves.

dive simulator: A training center for operating submarines.

Enduring Freedom: A major global campaign against terrorism.

Executive Department: The department that runs a submarine.

merchant ships: Unarmed vessels used to carry cargo.

nuclear: Creating energy by splitting atoms or bashing them together.

periscope: A tube with mirrors for observing the ocean surface.

predecessor: An earlier version of something.

radar: A detection system that works by using radio waves.

SEALS: U.S. Navy special forces; "SEALs" stands for Sea, Air, and Land.

sonar: A tracking system that uses sound to detect activity.

tactical: Relating to smaller, short-term operations against the enemy.

Trident: A ballistic missile armed with a nuclear warhead.

U-boat: Short for "Unterseeboot," a German submarine.

warhead: The explosive part of a missile.

watch: A naval word for a shift, or a period spent at work.

FURTHER READING

BOOKS

Abramson, Andra Serlin. *Submarines Up Close*. Sterling, 2008.

Adamson, Thomas K. *U.S. Navy Submarines* (Blazers: Military Vehicles). Capstone Press, 2006.

Bodden, Valerie. *Submarines* (Built for Battle). Creative Education, 2012.

Graham, Ian. *You Wouldn't Want to Be in the First Submarine: An Undersea Expedition You'd Rather Avoid*. Children's Press, 2008.

Mallard, Neil. *Submarine* (Eyewitness Books). DK Children, 2003.

Stone, Lynn M. *Submarines* (Fighting Forces on the Sea). Rourke Publishing, 2005.

Teitelbaum, Michael. *Submarines: Underwater Stealth* (Mighty Military Machines). Enslow Publications, 2009.

WEBSITES

http://americanhistory.si.edu/subs
Smithsonian Institution website on Fast Attacks and Boomers: Submarines in the Cold War.

http://www.navy.mil/navydata/ships/subs/subs.asp
U.S. Navy site marking 100 years of the submarine force, with fact files and images of submarines.

http://inventors.about.com/od/sstartinventions/a/submarines/htm
About.com guide to the history and design of submarines.

http://military.discovery.com/technology/vehicles/submarines/submarines-intro.html
Military Channel website listing Top 10 submarines of all time.

INDEX